GENESIS

BIBLESTUDY CROSSWORDS

BOB MEISTER

WESTBOW
PRESS®
A DIVISION OF THOMAS NELSON
& ZONDERVAN

WestBow Press books may be ordered through booksellers or by contacting:

WestBow Press
A Division of Thomas Nelson & Zondervan
1663 Liberty Drive
Bloomington, IN 47403
www.westbowpress.com
1 (866) 928-1240

Because of the dynamic nature of the Internet, any web addresses or links contained in this book may have changed since publication and may no longer be valid. The views expressed in this work are solely those of the author and do not necessarily reflect the views of the publisher, and the publisher hereby disclaims any responsibility for them.

Any people depicted in stock imagery provided by Getty Images are models, and such images are being used for illustrative purposes only.
Certain stock imagery © Getty Images.

Scripture quotations taken from the New American Standard Bible® (NASB),
Copyright © 1960, 1962, 1963, 1968, 1971, 1972, 1973,
1975, 1977, 1995 by The Lockman Foundation
Used by permission. www.Lockman.org

ISBN: 978-1-9736-8415-2 (sc)
ISBN: 978-1-9736-8414-5 (e)

Print information available on the last page.

WestBow Press rev. date: 02/20/2020

CONTENTS

BIBLESTUDY CROSSWORDS

Learning God's Word!

The purpose of BibleStudy CrossWords is to help people retain God's Word and go deeper into its meaning. Our hope is that our puzzles will become tools to make scripture an integral part of your life and increase your faith in Jesus Christ. The NIV Bible is the only reference where you will find the answers to the across and down questions. Solving the puzzles is a three-step process:

1. Read the designated verses in an NIV Bible. If you take your time reading you will remember more detail; if you read more than once you will retain more of the storyline and specific words demanded by the puzzles. You will find that you read differently when reading to remember than just doing a casual read.

2. Select from the *Down* and *Across* questions you prefer based on how the puzzle is developing and fill in the answers as best you can. You may consider selecting questions that already have one or more letters filled in to help formulate a correct answer.

3. Check your answers with an NIV Bible after you have gone through all the questions. Every answer will consist of a specific word used in the designated Bible verse. If there are questions you were unable to answer, read the corresponding verse and fill in the correct answer. This is the *study* part of BibleStudy CrossWords.

CrossWords for Bible Study

HOME STUDY – set aside one day each week to read the designated chapters for a puzzle. Read the chapters *slowly* at least twice before attempting to solve the puzzle. Begin by selecting the questions that appear to be the easiest to answer and continue as letter-clues help you to answer more questions. Finally, refer to the designated chapter and verse to find the correct words to unanswered questions.

CLASSROOM – Many study formats are possible in a group setting. The most popular with churches is to bring the books to class after doing the puzzles at home. Class-time is devoted to discussing context surrounding the most meaningful and difficult questions to answer. Others elect to do the puzzles in class in a competitive team format.

The puzzles vary in difficulty. Try not to become frustrated by the more difficult; going back to the Bible for answers is the most important part of the learning process.

CrossWords

GENESIS 1-4

Creation

"Lift up your eyes on high,
and see who has created these stars,
The one who leads forth their host by number,
He calls them all by name;
Because of the greatness of His might
and the strength of His power
not one of them is missing."

Isaiah 40:26 NASB

Non-believers say that *creation* came from something that already existed. Christians hold the same belief – that God existed before creation and is the source for all that exists and has authority over everything. It is His world; everything in it including you and me, the cars we drive, our homes and clothing. Everything has been created directly by God or from the raw materials He provides.

The same is true of the universe. Scientists say the universe is over 14-billion years old and the earth was created over 4-billion years ago by some sort of big-bang. But to say that all this just evolved somehow and continues to function perfectly is not believable and takes more faith than to believe in a perfect and Holy God.

The first chapters of Genesis are an accounting of God's six-days of creation. Included is the introduction of obedience and the origin of sin when man refused to obey God's simple instruction not to pick fruit from a specific tree in the Garden of Eden. Since then however, He has provided a way for us to attain His forgiveness.

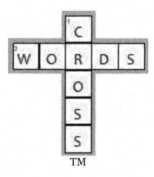

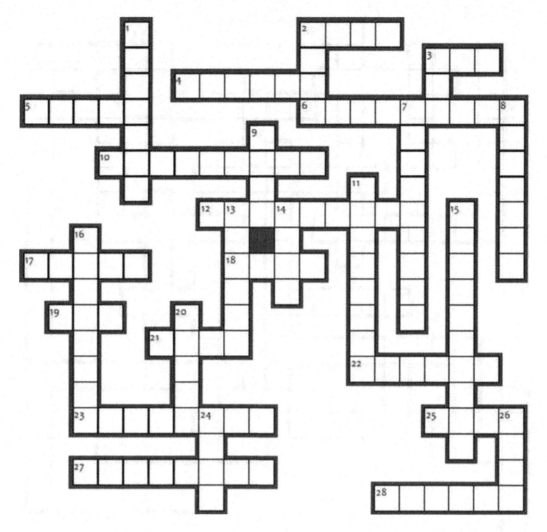

Across Genesis 1-2

2. The second type of animals created? 1:24
3. What name did God give to light? 1:5
4. God made this so man would not be alone. 2:18
5. What did God set in the sky to give earth light? 1:16
6. The name of one of the trees God planted. 2:9
10. When did God create the heavens and the earth? 1-1
12. God created these to live in the water. 1:21
17. The second thing created on the fourth day. 1:20
18. What did God call the gathered waters? 1:10
19. What God made immediately after the animals? 1-26
21. How did God describe all he had made? 1:31
22. What did God create on the fourth day? 1:14
23. What was over the surface of the deep? 1:2
25. God gave green plants for what purpose? 1:30
26. What did God use to form man? 2:7
27. In the beginning the earth was __and empty. 1:2
28. Who was hovering over the waters? 1:2

Down Genesis 1-2

1. God did this to the seventh day to make it holy. 2:3
2. The purpose for putting man in the garden. 2:15
3. The result of man-eating fruit of the second tree? 2:17
7. The first animals God created on the sixth day. 1:24
8. What separated the waters? 1:6
9. For this a man will leave his father and mother. 2:24
11. What God asked man and woman to be. 1:28
13. What did God do on the seventh day? 2:2
14. What name did God give to man? 2:20
15. The last thing God created on the third day. 1:11
16. God took this action to give man life. 2:7
20. God made this from man's rib. 2:22
24. God planted a garden here. 2:8

Bible Study CrossWords

Genesis 1-2

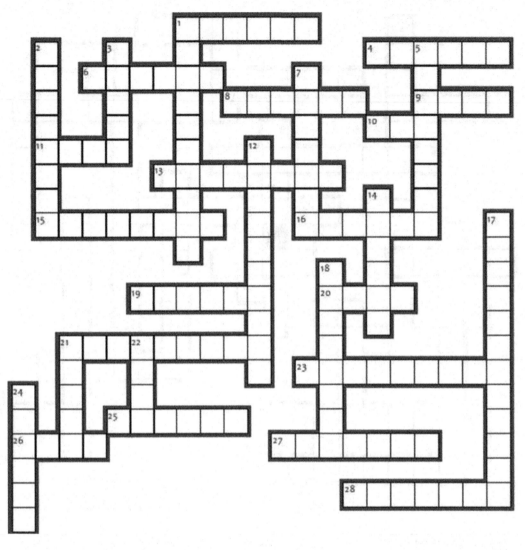

Across	Genesis 3-4
1.	Garden location of the forbidden fruit? 3:3
4.	God told Adam this was to be his food. 3:18
6.	God put this between the animal and the woman. 3:15
8.	Cain did this to Abel. 4:8
9.	Name of the first son born to Adam and his wife? 4:1
10.	What would happen if the women disobeyed God? 3:4
11.	What was the name of Adam's third son? 4:25
13.	What guarded the east side of the Garden? 3:24
15.	The woman said she was___by the serpent. 3:13
16.	God cursed this because of Adam's disobedience. 3:17
19.	This could be gained from forbidden fruit___ . 3:6
20.	The name of the second son born to Adam's wife. 4:2
21.	Abel brought God fat portions from what animals? 4:4
23.	God said anyone who kills Cain would suffer this. 4:15
25.	Abel's work was to keep these. 4:2
26.	God put this on Cain to protect him. 4:15
27.	This was the craftiest animal God made. 3:1
28.	What was God doing in the garden? 3:8

Down	Genesis 3-4
1.	Who was the father of Lamech? 4:18
2.	God said man was___from the garden. 3:23
3.	What was the name of Cain's son?4:17
5.	If Cain would do what is right, he would be___ . 4:7
7.	Type of sword used to guard the tree of life? 3:24
12.	Cain said he could not bear this. 4:13
14.	God did this to the serpent. 3:14
17.	When would woman have increased pain? 3:16
18.	Cain's punishment was to become a restless___. 4:12
21.	God did not look with___on Cain's offering. 4:5
22.	Abel kept flocks. What did Cain work? 4:2
24.	Who married two women? 4:19

Bible Study CrossWords

Genesis 3-4

GENESIS 5-11
Noah

"Then the Lord said to Noah, 'Enter the ark,
you and all your household;
for you alone I have seen to be righteous
before me in this time."

When God said let us make man in our own image, in our likeness, it was the first hint of a triune God who became the pattern for our soul, spirit and intelligence. Unfortunately, the world in Noah's day became filled with evil, so God used a flood to cleanse the earth and used Noah and his family to give life on earth a new start.

Imagine, even with all the resources available to use in this day, getting an assignment from God as Noah did to build an ark that is 300-cubits x 50-cubits x 30-cubits (that is about 450-feet long x 75-feet wide x 45-feet high) and fill it with two of every kind of creature on earth along with enough food to sustain them and his family.

The next assignment, was for Noah's three sons and their wives, to give life a fresh start; "from these the whole earth was populated." Finally, God made a covenant, marked by the appearance of a rainbow, that He would never again use a flood to destroy the earth,

TM

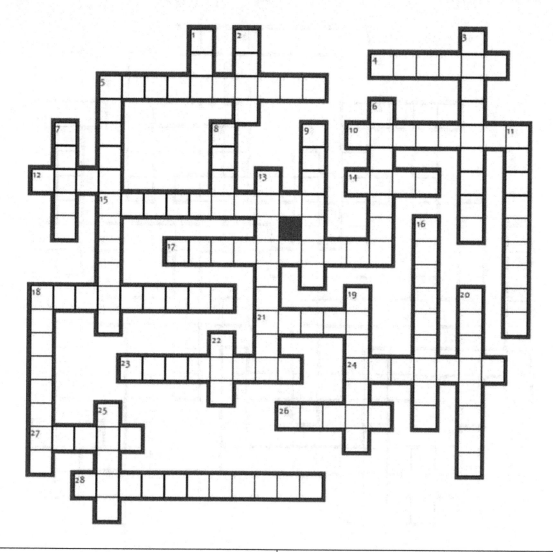

Across   Genesis 5-8

4. On what mountain did the ark come to rest? 8:4
5. The ____ of the heavens were opened. 7:11
10. Who were the "Heroes of old, men of renown? 6:4
12. What happened to Adam at age 930? 5:5
14. Name of Adam's first son. 5:3
15. What trait did God observe about men? 6:5
17. Who died at age 969? 5:27
18. The people were ____ in their ways 6:12
21. How many days and nights did it rain? 7:4
23. What were the animals to do after the flood? 8-17
24. How did the waters react to the wind? 8:1
26. The name of Seth's first son. 5:6
27. The first bird sent to check the water and earth? 8:7
28. What day of the month did the ark come to rest? 8:4

Down   Genesis 5-8

1. In whose likeness was man created. 5:1
2. Who was the father of Japheth? 5:32
3. Who was Jared's father? 5:15
5. What did God use to destroy life on earth? 6:17
6. During what month did the ark come to rest? 8:4
7. What leaf did the dove bring back to the ark? 8:11
8. What did God use to recede the waters? 8:1
9. God ____ the people he created. 5:2
11. What were covered with water? 7:20
13. How were the "daughters of men" viewed? 6:2
16. Noah was described as righteous and ____. 6:9
18. God wiped every __ from the face of the earth. 7:4
19. What wood was used to build the ark? 6:14
20. What did God establish with Noah? 6:18
22. How many hundred years old was Noah? 7:11
25. How many of each animal did Noah take? 7:2

Bible Study CrossWords

Genesis 5-8

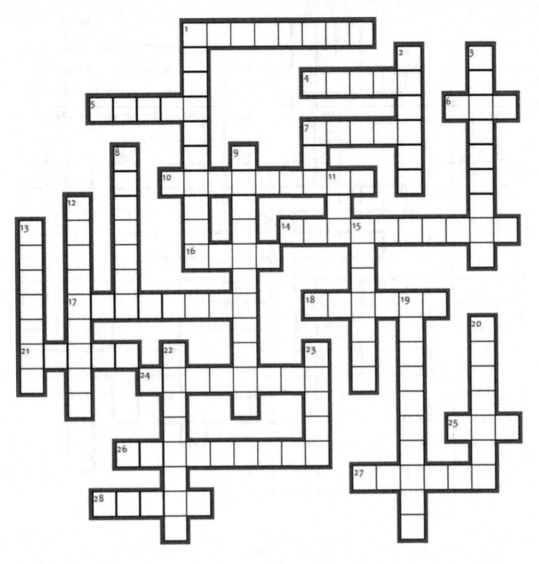

Across	**Genesis 9-11**
1.	God did this to the language of the world. 11:9
4.	The name of Abram's wife. 11:29
5.	Where the Lord confused the world's language. 11:9
6.	What did men use for mortar? 11:3
7.	What did the men build to reach the heavens? 11:4
10.	A food restriction was meat containing _____. 9:4
14.	What God gave to Noah and his sons as food.9:3
16.	Canaan became the slave of this person. 9:26
17.	What did Noah plant after leaving the ark? 9:20
18.	Which of his sons did Noah curse? 9:25
21.	Who was Abram's father? 11:27
24.	Noah's sons were told to be ____ to increase in number. 9:1
25.	Who was Terah's grandson? 11:31
26.	The people were ____ over the earth. 11:9
27.	What the men used to build the city. 11:3
28.	Who was the father of Lot? 11:27

Down	**Genesis 9-11**
1.	The Philistines came from this clan. 10:14
2.	Who grew to be a mighty warrior? 10:8
3.	The people who lived in Ur. 11:31
7.	How many sons were born to Eber? 10:25
8.	This center was a part of Nimrod's kingdom. 10:10
9.	God made a covenant with Noah and his ___. 9:9
11.	How many languages were in the world? 11:1
12.	Noah's appearance after drinking wine. 9:21
13.	Who was told to live in the tents of Shem? 9:27
15.	The sign of God's covenant. 9:13
19.	God demands this from a man who kills another. 9:6
20.	What spread over the earth after the flood? 10:32
22.	Who was Shem's first son? 11:10
23.	God wouldn't destroy the earth this way again. 9:11

Bible Study CrossWords

Genesis 9-11

GENESIS 12-23

Abraham

"And He said, 'Take now your only son, whom you
love, Isaac, and to the land of Moriah;
and offer him there as a burnt offering
on one of the mountains of which I will tell you."
Genesis 22:2 NASB

God did not want Abraham's son to die. He was rebuilding His world; people were once again engaged in sin and God needed someone in which He could have complete confidence. Abraham was tested to determine his love and devotion to God, his obedience and faith. He commanded Abraham to sacrifice Isaac, his only son.

Abraham remained obedient demonstrating that he loved God more than his only son, showing complete faith in God and His perfect timing. When Isaac asked where the lamb was for the burnt offering in faith, Abraham told Isaac that God himself would provide the lamb for the burnt offering. He did.

Later, God spoke to Abraham with the promise of a reward, which was that all the nations of the earth would come from his seed and they would be blessed because he had obeyed God's voice.

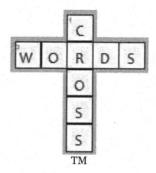

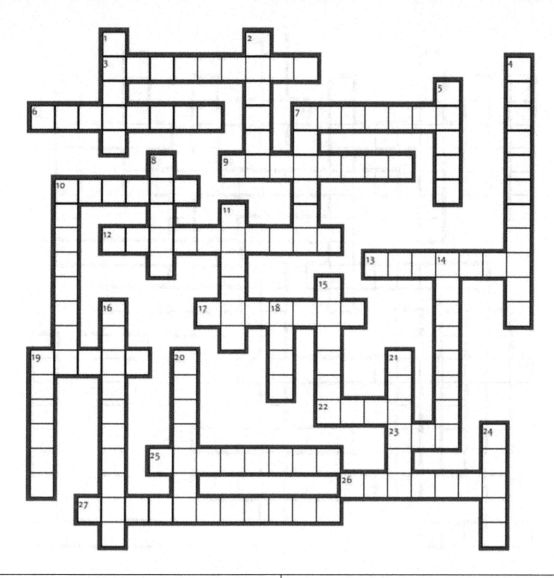

Across	Genesis 12-15
3.	God gave the land of Canaan to Abram's _____. 12:7
6.	Birsha was king and leader of what army? 14:2
7.	What Abram accepted from the King of Sodom 14:23
9.	Abram said he and Lot were _____. 13:8
10.	Abram, his wife and Lot set out for what land? 12:5
12.	What happened between the herdsmen? 13:7
13.	Where was the great tree of Moreh located? 12:6
17.	Abram's financial status after leaving Egypt. 13:2
19.	God told Abram to count these. 15:5
22.	God said a son from Abram would be his _____ 15:4
23.	Where Abram went to find Lot. 14:14
25.	Hobah is north of what city? 14:15
26.	What were the men of Sodom doing? 13:13
27.	Who was the king of Salem? 14:18

Down	Genesis 12-15
1.	Lot pitched his tents near what city? 13:12
2.	Abram's wife said she was his _____. 12:13
4.	Who was king of Elam? 14:1
5.	Where did Abram go to escape the famine? 12:10
7.	God promised to make Abram a great _____. 12:2
8.	What city did Abram leave to begin his journey? 12:4
10.	The Lord made this with Abram. 15:18
11.	Where did Abram pitch his tent? 12:8
14.	Abram was concerned he had none of these. 15:3
15.	The king of Sodom met Abram in this valley. 14:17
16.	The Canaanites and _____ were living near Bethel. 13:7
18.	God said Abram could have all this he could see. 13:15
19.	In what valley did the kings join forces? 14:3
20.	Who treated Abram well because of his wife? 12:16
21.	Lot headed toward what plain to live. 13:11
24.	Where did Abram go with his wife and Lot? 13:1

Across   **Genesis 16-17**

9.   Who did Hagar say she was running away from? 16:8
10. God asked Abram to walk and be ____. 17:1
11. What was the name of Sarai's maidservant? 16:1
12. The sign of God's covenant with Abraham. 17:11
14. Who did Sarai blame for her suffering? 16:5
15. How did God refer to himself to Abram? 17:1
16. Ishmael's age when circumcised. 17:25
19. How many rulers would Ishmael father? 17:20
23. How many years did Abram live in Canaan? 16:3
25. A male who would be cut off from his people. 17:14
26. What new name did God give to Abram? 17:5
27. What was the nationality of Sarai's maidservant? 16:1
28. Where did the angel of the Lord find Hagar? 16:7
29. Abraham ____ when told he would be a father. 17:17

Down   **Genesis 16-17**

1.   What was the new name given to Sarai? 17:15
2.   What did God confirm with Abram? 17:2
3.   What land did God give to Abraham? 17:8
4.   Hagar was to do this to her mistress. 16:9
5.   The name of Abraham and Sarah's son? 17:19
6.   Sarai did this to Hagar. 16:6
7.   God____said would come from Sarah. 17:16
8.   What was beside the road to Shur? 16:7
13. The angel told Hagar to give her son this name. 16:11
17. Ishmael would live in ____toward his brothers. 16:12
18. Hagar was told that her _____ would increase. 16:10
20. How long was the covenant with Abraham? 17:7
21. How old was Abram when he saw the Lord? 17:1
22. Abram fell _____ when he saw the Lord. 17:3
24. Hagar _____ when sleeping with Abram. 16:4

Bible Study CrossWords

Genesis 16-17

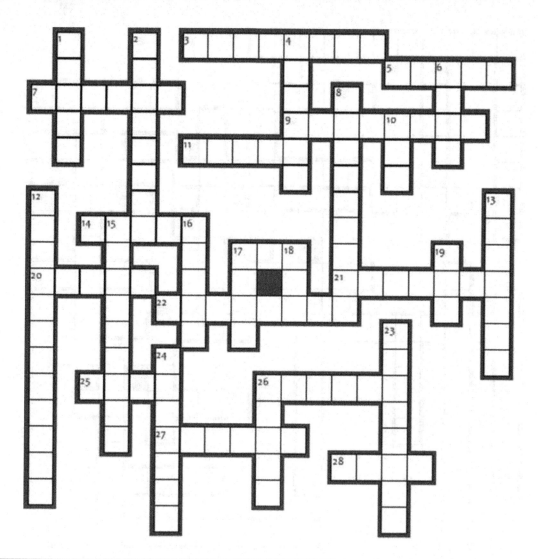

Across	Genesis 18-20

3. How did Sarah refer to having a child? 18:12
5. How did Abraham greet the men? 18:2
7. Sarah was the daughter of Abraham's ____ 20:12
9. How many shekels did Sarah's brother get? 20:16
11. How many men visited Abraham? 18:2
14. How did God come to Abimelech? 20:3
17. Who was sitting in the gateway to Sodom? 19:1
20. The Lord asked Abraham why Sarah did this. 18:13
21. All these would be blessed through Abraham. 18:18

22. The description of Sodom and Gomorrah's sins. 18:20
25. Name of the town where Lot fled. 19:22
26. Where did the angels want to spend the night? 19:2
27. Lot's wife became a ____ of salt. 19:26
28. Name of Lot's oldest daughter's son. 19:37

Down	Genesis 18-20

1. This was not in the bread the angels ate. 19:3
2. The daughters wanted to ____ their family line. 19:34
4. Who did Abraham say Sarah was? 20:2
6. What did the daughters give Lot to drink? 19:33
8. Where were Lot and his wife told to flee? 19:17
10. What did the Sodom men want with the Angels? 19:5
12. Sarah was past the age of ____. 18:11
13. All nations would be ____through Abraham. 18:18
15. Abraham asked God if the ____would be killed with the wicked? 18:25
16. Where did Abraham pitch his tent? 18:1
17. Sarah did this because she was afraid. 18:15
18. How many angels went to Sodom? 19:1
19. Who kept Abimelech from sinning? 20:6
23. The condition of both Lot's daughters. 19:36
24. God told Abimelech Abraham was a ____? 20:7
26. Abraham asked Sarah for three ____ of flour. 18:6

Bible Study
CrossWords

Genesis 18-20

~ 15 ~

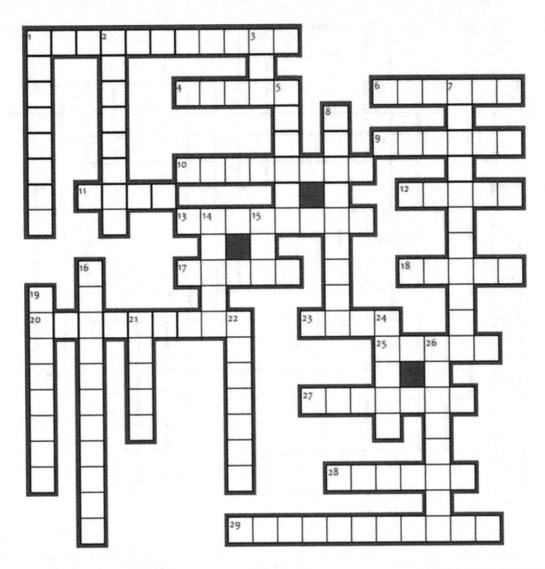

Across — Genesis 21

1. Abraham stayed in the land of the ____. 21:34
4. Number of lambs Abraham gave Abimelech. 21:28
6. What did God hear Hagar's son doing? 21:17
9. What did Hagar's son become in the dessert? 21:20
10. The Lord did to Sarah what he had ____. 21:1
11. What Hagar saw when God opened her eyes. 21:19
12. Who did God tell Abraham to listen to? 21:12
13. Phicol asked Abraham to show him this. 21:23
17. What did Hagar run out of in the desert? 21:15
18. What happened the day Isaac was weaned? 21:8
20. Who did Abraham make a treaty with? 21:27
23. Beersheba got its name because of this. 21:31
25. Who spoke to Hagar from heaven? 21:17
27. Who gave sheep and cattle to Abimelech. 21:27
28. Who commanded Abimelech's forces. 21:22
29. What happened to Isaac when eight days old? 21:4

Down — Genesis 21

1. God enabled Sarah to be like this. 21:2
2. Sarah's reaction to God's blessing. 21:6
3. What kind of lambs did Abimelech get? 21:29
5. God said he would make Ishmael into this. 21:13
7. Ishmael would not share this with Isaac. 21:10
8. Hagar and Ishmael wandered in this desert. 21:14
14. The name of Sarah's son. 21:3
15. Hagar feared this would happen to her son. 21:16
16. This person's son would become a nation. 21:13
19. The kind of tree Abraham planted in Beersheba. 21:33
21. Hagar's son's wife was from here. 21:21
22. Abraham's age when Isaac was born. 21:5
24. Who Abraham sent away with food and water. 21:14
26. The Lord was ____ to Sarah. 21:1

Across	Genesis 22-23

3. God asked Abraham to ____ Isaac. 22:2
5. "Bethuel became the father of ____" 22:23
6. The angel called to Abraham from ____. 22:15
7. Name of Abraham's brother. 22:20
8. Abraham said ____ would provide the lamb. 22:8
11. Abraham was blessed because he ____. 22:18
12. Where did Sarah die? 23:2
13. Isaac asked where the ____ was for the offering. 22:7
15. Abraham wanted to buy the cave of ____. 23:9
18. Who stopped the slaying of Isaac? 22:11
20. Abraham paid 400 ____ of silver. 23:15
25. Nahor had ____ sons. 22:23
26. What did Abraham sacrifice? 22:13
27. Who lived to be 127 years old? 23:1
28. Abraham was blessed with ____. 22:17

Down	Genesis 22-23

1. Abraham called the place The Lord Will ____. 22:14
2. Abraham went to ____ after the sacrifice. 22:19
4. Reumah was Nahor's ____. 22:24
9. Abraham used this to carry the wood. 22:3
10. Abraham traveled with Isaac and two _. 22:19
14. What did Abraham build to hold the wood? 22:9
15. Abraham was told, "____ is also a mother." 22:20
16. Abraham spoke to the ____ about a burial site. 23:3
17. Abraham cut wood for the . 22:3
19. Abraham was ____ by God. 22:1
21. What did Abraham not withhold from God? 22:12
22. God sent Abraham to the region of ____. 22:2
23. Aram's father. 22:21
24. Who owned the field in Machpelah? 23:17

Bible Study
CrossWords
Genesis 22-23

GENESIS 24-36

Isaac and Jacob

"But God said, 'No, but Sarah your wife shall bear you a son, and you shall call him Isaac; and I will establish my covenant with him for an everlasting covenant for his descendants after him."
Genesis 17:19 NASB

The story of Isaac and Jacob is a continuation of Abraham's heritage, God's plan for the nations on earth and further demonstration of God's control and timing.

God selected Rebekah as Isaac's wife and blessed her with twin boys, Jacob and Esau, who would eventually become two conflicting nations; the Israelites and the Edomites.

"And the Lord said to her, two nations are in your womb; and two peoples will be separated from your body; and one people shall be stronger than the other; and the older shall serve the younger."
Genesis 17:19 NASB

God eventually changed Jacob's name to Israel. This was fulfillment of God's promise to create a great nation through which he would bless the world. Ten of Jacob's twelve sons became the heads of tribes named after them.

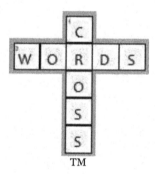

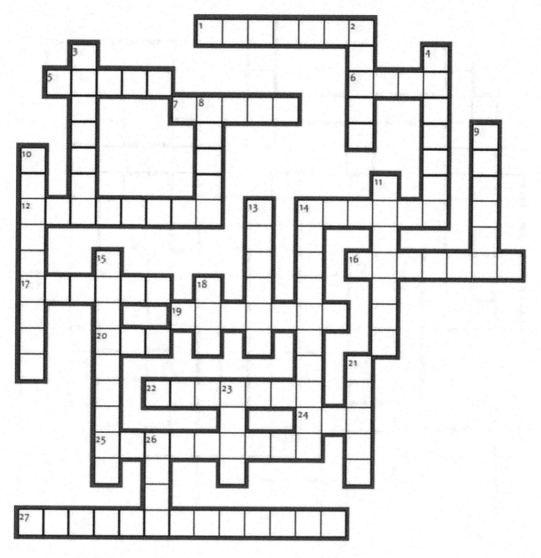

Across · Genesis 24

1. Who was Rebekah's father? 24:24
5. Where did the servant go to find Isaac's wife? 24:10
6. The weight of the gold nose ring. 24:22
7. What did the camels do near the well? 24:11
12. What did Isaac do when he went to the field? 24:63
14. The servant took ten of these on his trip. 24:10
16. How did the servant describe Abraham? 24:35
17. What was Rebekah asked to do for 10-days. 24:55
19. Who offered the servant a drink? 24:15
20. Who brought Abraham out of his native land? 24:7
22. Who oversaw all Abraham had. 24:2
24. The servant refused this until telling his story. 24:33
25. Isaac's wife was to come from his ___. 24:4
27. Rebekah's relationship to Abraham's brother. 24:48

Down · Genesis 24 Genesis 24

2. Who was Rebekah's brother. 24:29
3. What happened to Isaac and Rebekah? 24:67
4. The servant stayed with his ___ relatives. 24:27
8. This person traveled with Rebekah. 24:59
9. Who was the wife of Nahor? 24:15
10. Rebekah ___ Isaac after his mother's death. 24:67
11. What did the servant give to Rebekah? 24:53
13. What did the servant do near the spring? 24:12
14. Who was Abraham living among? 24:3
15. Who of the town came to the spring for water. 24:13
18. How many shekels did two bracelets weigh? 24:22
21. What did Rebekah give the camels? 24:19
23. What did Rebekah cover herself with? 24:65
26. Who gave Abraham all he possessed? 24:35

Bible Study CrossWords

Genesis 24

Bible Study CrossWords

Genesis 25-26

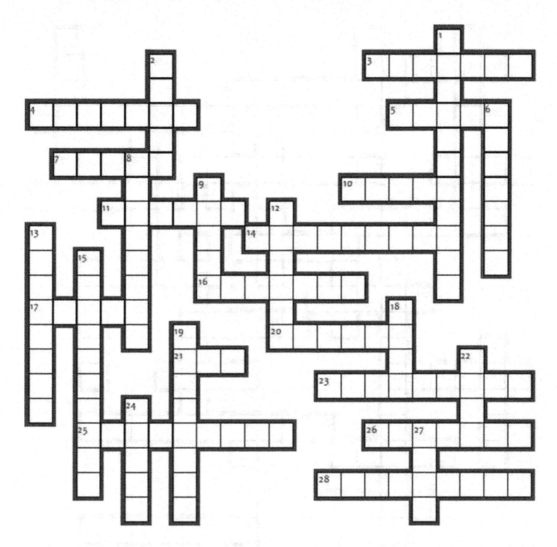

Across   **Genesis 27-28**

3.   Who overheard Isaac and Esau talking? 27:5
4.   What did Jacob wear of Esau's? 27:15
5.   Who did Rebekah conspire with? 27:6
7.   Rebekah prepared a meal from these for Isaac. 27:9
10.   What did Jacob's clothes smell like? 27:27
11.   Where did Jacob have his dream? 28:19
14.   Jacob told Isaac he was his ____. 27:19
16.   What Esau was doing before seeing Isaac. 27:30
17.   Rebekah told Jacob to let this fall on her. 27:13
20.   Isaac questioned if Jacob was ___Esau. 27:21
21.   The former name for the city Bethel. 28:19
23.   People would be blessed by Jacob's ____. 28:14
25.   What Jacob used to cover his hands. 27:16
26.   Isaac ____ Jacob because he had hairy hands. 27:23
28.   These women displeased Isaac. 28:8

Down   **Genesis 27-28**

1.   Jacob's __ would be like the dust of the earth. 28:14
2.   What Esau wanted his father to do to him. 27:38
6.   Isaac told Esau he would serve this person. 27:40
8.   Isaac's reaction to being deceived by Jacob. 27:33
9.   Jacob vowed to give God a ____ of all he had. 28:22
12.   Esau's reaction to loosing Jacob's blessing. 27:34
13.   Jacob feared a curse for doing this to Isaac. 27:12
15.   Esau accused Jacob of taking this from him. 27:36
18.   Isaac's ____ were weak. 27:1
19.   Isaac wanted to give Esau this before dying. 27:4
22.   Isaac asked Jacob for this thinking he was Esau.27:26
24.   Jacob's hands felt this way to Isaac. 27:23
27.   Who did Isaac ask to hunt for him? 27:3

Bible Study
CrossWords

Genesis 27-28

Across	Genesis 29-30
4.	The name of Leah's third son. 29:34
5.	What Jacob used to streak or spot the animals? 30:37
7.	Laban ___ and kissed Jacob 29:13
10.	What kind of animals went to Laban? 30:42
11.	Jacob was ___ by Laban. 29:25
12.	The name of Leah's first son. 29:32
13.	Leah made Rachel feel this way. 30:1
15.	Where were the shepherds from? 29:4
18.	Who became Jacob's second wife? 29:28
20.	How many flocks of sheep were near the well? 29:2
21.	Leah ___ Jacob to sleep with her. 30:16
23.	The name of Jacob's fourth wife. 30:8
24.	Laban gave ___ to Jacob instead of Rachel. 29:23
25.	Separating the animals made Jacob ___. 30:43
27.	The name of Leah's fourth son. 29:35
28.	What Jacob did to make Rachel weep. 29:11
29.	Jacob journeyed to the land of the ___ people. 29:1

Down	Genesis 29-30
1.	Jacob made ___ flocks for he and Laban. 30:40
2.	Jacob did this to get Rachel as his wife. 29:27
3.	Simeon got his name because Leah was not ___. 29:33
6.	Jacob offered to work ___ years to marry Rachel. 29:18
8.	Who was Jacob mother? 29:12
9.	Who became Dan's mother? 30:6
14.	Jacob's wages were goats and _. 30:32
16.	What kind of plants did Reuben give Leah? 30:14
17.	Rachel worked as a ___. 29:9
19.	Who was Nahor's grandson? 29:5
22.	The name of Leah's daughter. 30:21
26.	This blocked the mouth of the well. 29:3

Bible Study *CrossWords*

Genesis 29-30

Across   Genesis 31-32

4. In what season did Jacob dream of livestock? 31:10
6. Laban asked Jacob to make a ___ with him. 31:44
9. Jacob ran away with Laban's ___. 31:26
11. What did Jacob hurt when wrestling. 32:25
12. What was God between Laban and Jacob? 31:50
14. How many sons did Jacob have? 32:22
17. Name of Jacob's camp after seeing angels? 32:2
20. Jacob said that Laban had ___ him. 31:7
23. Jacob said God took away Laban's ___. 31:9
25. Who did not allow Laban to harm Jacob? 31:7
26. Where did Rachel hide Laban's gods? 31:34
27. Where did Jacob take his livestock and Family? 31:18
28. What Jacob did with God to change his name. 32:28

Down   Genesis 31-32

1. How many years had Jacob lived with Laban? 31:41
2. Jacob felt this because of God's kindness. 32:10
3. Laban chased Jacob to the hill country of ___. 31:23
5. Who should share in Laban's wealth? 31:16
7. Jacob sent messengers to Esau in ___. 32:3
8. Where did Jacob see God face to face? 32:30
10. What did Laban accuse Jacob of stealing? 31:30
13. How many times were Jacob's wages changed? 31:7
15. The name of Jacob's brother. 32:3
16. Jacob was accused of taking this from Laban. 31:1
18. Jacob saw Laban's ___ toward him had changed. 31:2
19. Until when did Jacob wrestle with the man? 32:24
21. What did Jacob call the heap of stones? 31:47
22. Who stole Laban's household gods? 31:19
24. What new name was given to Jacob? 32:28

Bible Study CrossWords

Genesis 31-32

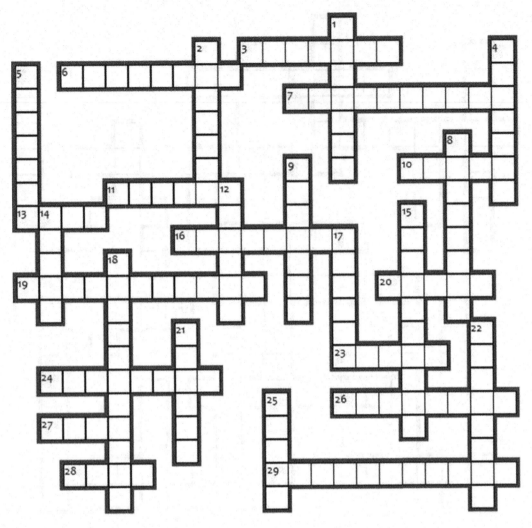

Across	Genesis 33-34
3.	Where Jacob went to build a place for himself. 33:17
6.	Sheshem needed approval from this group. 34:20
7.	Jacob's sons felt Dinah was treated like this. 34:31
10.	Jacob's sons took the city's children and ___. 34:29
11.	Simeon and Levi used these to kill Sheshem. 34:26
13.	Every ___ in the city was circumcised. 34:24
16.	Jacob's sons' ___ seemed good to Hamor. 34:18
19.	How Jacob's sons spoke to Sheshem. 34:13
20.	How many times did Jacob bow before Esau? 33:3
23.	Name of Jacob and Leah's daughter. 34:1
24.	What Dinah's brothers to the city. 34:25
26.	Esau told Jacob to keep what you have for ___. 33:9
27.	Sheshem wanted Dinah as his___. 34:4
28.	How many hundred men were with Esau? 33:1
29.	Jacob's sons insisted Hamor's sons be ___. 34:14

Down	Genesis 33-34
1.	Sheshem was most ___ in Hamor's household. 34:19
2.	Jacob heard this had happed to his daughter. 34:5
4.	What Esau reluctantly accepted from Jacob. 33:11
5.	David camped within sight of this city. 33:18
8.	Esau ran to Jacob and did this to him. 33:4
9.	The townsmen's response to intermarriage. 34:23
12.	Jacob had to move ___ to save the animals. 33:14
14.	What did Jacob set up at El Elohe? 33:20
15.	Hamor wanted Jacob's family and his to do this. 34:9
17.	What Jacob's sons did to the city. 34:27
18.	Jacob's sons' description of what Sheshem did. 34:7
21.	Jacob's sons' actions made him feel like a ___. 34:30
22.	Sheshem did to Dinah. 34:2
25.	Sheshem said he would pay any ___ for Dinah. 34:12

Bible Study CrossWords

Genesis 33-34

Across   **Genesis 35-36**

1. Rachel had great difficulty with this. 35:17
7. Who lived 180 years? 35:28
9. Another name for Bethel. 35:6
10. Israel was to be ___ and increase in number. 35:11
14. Who lived in the hill country of Seir? 36:9
15. Esau's wives came from here. 36:2
16. Jacob was to build an alter to ___. 35:1
19. The name of Hadad's city. 36:39
22. What did Rachel name her son? 35:18
23. Jacob told his family to ___ themselves. 35:2
26. Original owner of the land given to Israel. 35:12
27. Who did Rueben sleep with? 35:22
28. Where did God tell Jacob to settle? 35:1

Down   **Genesis 35-36**

2. Jacob's new name from God. 35:10
3. Who was the firstborn of Jacob? 35:23
4. Esau moved this and his family from Jacob. 36:6
5. Where Esau settled after leaving Jacob. 36:8
6. God said that ___ would come from Israel. 35:11
8. Jacob built this at Bethel to honor God. 35:14
10. Jacob's family gave him their ___ gods. 35:4
11. Another name for Esau. 36:1
12. The name Israel gave to Rachel's son. 35:18
13. Name of Leah's maidservant. 35:26
17. Name of Rebekah's nurse. 35:8
18. Who was Chief Korah's mother? 36:18
20. These would come from Israel's body. 35:11
21. Rachel was buried on the way to ___. 35:19
24. How many sons did Jacob have? 35:22
25. Jacob came home to his father in ___. 35:27

Bible Study
CrossWords

Genesis 35-36

GENESIS 37-50

Joseph

"You shall be over my house and according to your
command all my people shall do homage;
only in the throne will I be greater than you."
Genesis 41:40 NASB

Joseph was betrayed by his brothers, sold into slavery, exposed to sexual temptation, punished for doing what was right, endured a long imprisonment and was forgotten by those he helped.

It was his reliance on God that saw every situation he faced ultimately used for good. He demonstrated the value of relying on God when facing adversity and that what matters most is our response to problems.

After being sold as a slave by his brothers Joseph rose to lead one of the mightiest nations in the world. As the ruler of Egypt, he taught the people how to prepare for and survive a famine that might otherwise have destroyed their nation.

After being reunited with his brothers he forgave them and told them not to be distressed or be angry with themselves because what happened was all for the good and part of God's plan.

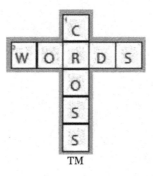

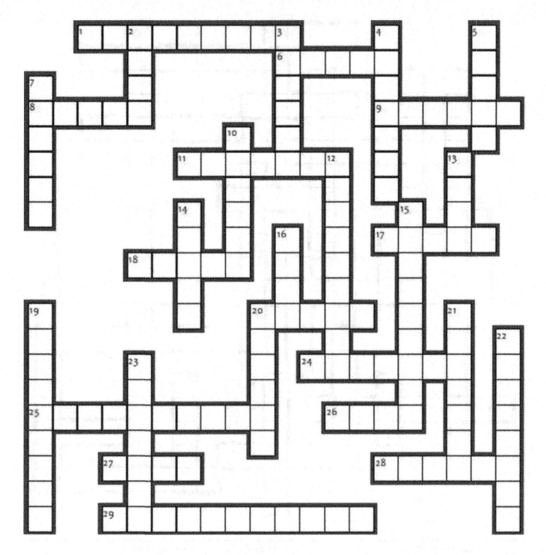

	Across	Genesis 37-38
1.	Judah said Tamar was more ___ than he. 38:26
6.	Judah went to stay with ___. 38:1
8.	Where did the merchants take Joseph? 37:28
9.	Where did Jacob live? 37:1
11.	Reuben tore his __when Joseph was missing. 37:29
17.	The name of Tamar's firstborn. 38:29
18.	Who made Tamar pregnant? 38:18
20.	Joseph's robe was dipped in ___. 37:31
24.	Joseph was sold for 20 ___ of silver. 37:28
25.	Who did Tamar look like with her face covered? 38:15
26.	Tamar gave birth to ___ boys. 38:27
27.	What did Tamar use as a disguise. 38:14
28.	Where did Judah go after his wife died. 38:12
29.	Who did Judah suggest selling Joseph to? 37:27

	Down	Genesis 37-38
2.	Judah promised this to sleep with Tamar. 38:17
3.	Judah's third son's name. 38:5
4.	Joseph was sent here to be with his brothers. 37:13
5.	Joseph's brothers hated him because of this. 37:8
7.	Which brother tried to rescue Joseph? 37:21
10.	Which son did Israel love the most? 37:3
12.	What did Jacob wear in mourning? 37:34
13.	What did Israel make for Joseph? 37:3
14.	Judah told Tamar to live as a ___. 38:11
15.	How old was Joseph? 37:2
16.	What Tamar wanted as a pledge from Judah. 38:18
19.	What Onan did not want to produce with Tamar 38:9
20.	How did Judah want Tamar to die? 38:24
21.	Where did Joseph brothers throw him? 37:24
22.	Who purchased Joseph from his brothers? 37:36
23.	To whose house did Tamar go to live. 38:11

Bible Study
CrossWords

Genesis 37-38

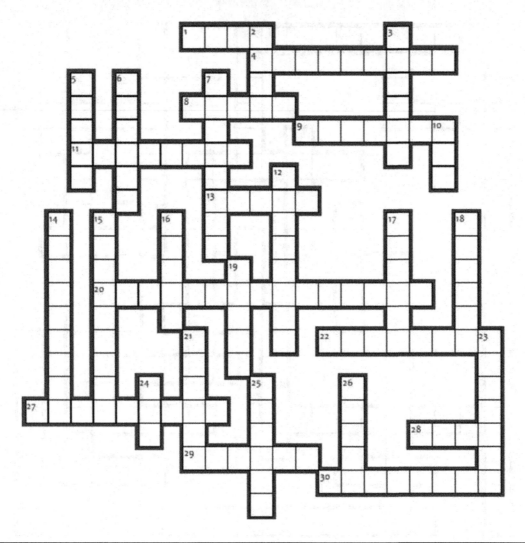

Across   Genesis 39-40

1.   Who gave Joseph success in everything? 39:3
4.   Joseph's position with Potiphar. 39:4
8.   How Pharaoh celebrated his birthday. 40:20
9.   What the baker dreamed he had on his head. 40:16
11. In prison two officials were ___ to Joseph. 40:4
13. An official who offended the king. 40:1
20. What did Joseph say belonged to God? 40:8
22. The Lord showed this to Joseph in prison. 39:21
27. How Joseph faired in his master's house. 39:2
28. What the cupbearer saw in his dream. 40:9
29. What Pharaoh did to the chief baker. 40:22
30. Potiphar was one of whose officials? 39:1

Down   Genesis 39-40

2.   What were the branches in Pharaoh's dream? 40:12
3.   Who put Joseph in charge of prisoners? 39:22
5.   What Joseph left in Potiphar's wife's hand. 39:12
6.   In anger, where did Potiphar put Joseph? 39:20
7.   Joseph asked the cupbearer to ___ him. 40:14
10. Joseph did not want to ___ against God. 39:9
12. Mood of officials the morning after dreaming. 40:6
14. The baker and who else offended the king. 40:1
15. Pharaoh was angry with these two men. 40:2
16. Number of branches on the vine. 40:10
17. Hearing his wife's story, the king with anger 39:19
18. What did the vine blossoms become? 40:10
19. Two officials each had this in prison. 40:5
21. Why Potiphar's household was blessed. 39:5
23. What the Lord gave Joseph in all he did. 39:23
24. Potiphar's wife wanted Joseph in ___ with her. 39:7
25. The cupbearer ___ to remember Joseph. 40:23
26. Joseph said birds would eat the baker's ___. 40:19

Bible Study *CrossWords*

Genesis 39-40

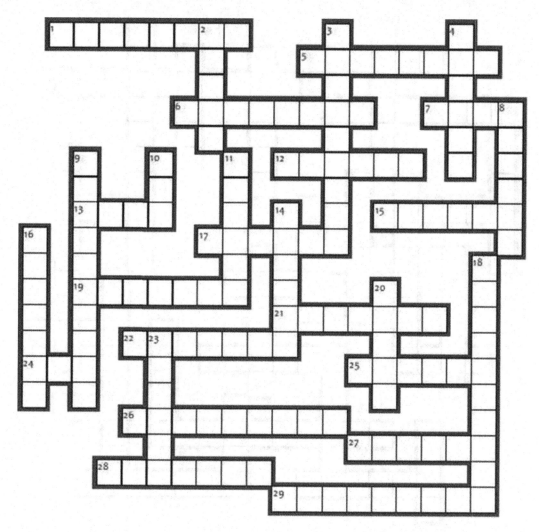

Across Genesis 41-42

1. Which brother did Joseph want to see? 42:15
5. The name of Joseph's first son. 41:51
6. Jacob feared this son being taken away. 42:36
7. What was Pharaoh's first dream about? 41:2
12. How old was Joseph? 41:46
13. What Joseph did with the grain during famine. 41:56
15. How Joseph described the expected famine. 41:31
17. Where Joseph stored the grain. 41:48
19. Grain was held in ___ for future use. 41:36
21. The name of Joseph's second son. 41:52
22. The brothers had to leave this behind to show their honesty. 42:34
24. How many brothers went to Egypt? 42:3
25. Who was put in charge of Egypt? 41:41
26. God would give Egypt seven years of this. 41:29
27. Which brother did Joseph have bound? 42:24
28. Joseph was brought to Pharaoh from here. 41:14
29. What did the thin grains do to the full heads? 41:7

Down Genesis 41-42

2. What Joseph called his brothers when they met 42:9
3. The first people who tried to solve the dreams. 41:8
4. Where did Joseph rank in-command? 41:43
8. The kind of ring Pharaoh gave Joseph. 41:42
9. Pharaoh was to look for a ___ wise man. 41:33
10. Who did Joseph say could interpret the dream? 41:16
11. What the ugly cows and thin grain meant. 41:27
14. What did one of the brothers find in his sack? 42:28
16. Who was the mother of Joseph's two sons? 41:50
18. How everyone felt when finding the pouches? 42:35
20. Who said he was deprived of his children? 42:36
23. Who wanted to be trusted by his father? 42:37

Bible Study CrossWords

Genesis 41-42

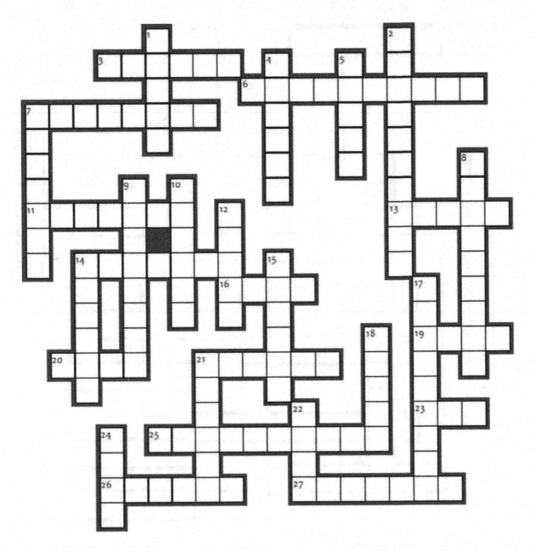

Across — Genesis 43-44

3. The brothers were accused of stealing ___. 44:8
6. Joseph's silver cup was used for ___. 44:5
7. Joseph was pleased when he saw ___. 43:16
11. Egyptians could not eat with ___. 43:32
13. Jacob's life was closely with Benjamin's life. 44:30
14. They made an appeal to Joseph's ___. 43:19
16. The men were seated in order of their ___. 43:33
19. The cup was found in Benjamin's ___. 44:12
20. Judah said Benjamin's brother was ___. 44:20
21. Joseph had asked questions about the ___. 43:7
23. What did Joseph put in Benjamin's sack? 44:2
25. How did the brothers feel in Joseph's house? 43:18
26. Joseph asked, "How is your aged ___?" 43:27
27. Judah said Joseph was equal to ___. 44:18

Down — Genesis 43-44

1. Judah would bear the ___ if Benjamin was not returned. 44:32
2. Eating with Hebrews was ___ to Egyptians. 43:32
4. Who did Joseph return to the brothers? 43:23
5. Judah asked Joseph not to be ___. 44:18
7. The brothers could not see Joseph again unless the brought their ___. 43:5
8. Judah asked how they could prove their ___. 44:16
9. Jacob repeated he felt this about the journey. 43:14
10. Who insisted the silver be returned? ___. 43:11
12. Who guaranteed their brothers safety? 43:8
14. The brothers feared they might become ___ 43:18
15. Judah offered to ___ with Joseph as a slave. 44:33
17. What kind of nuts did they bring to Joseph? 43:11
18. The brothers ___ before Joseph. 43:26
21. What was still severe in the land? 43:1
22. Joseph would ___ when he saw Benjamin. 43:30
24. Israel said to bring this to the "man." 43:11

Bible Study CrossWords

Genesis 43-44

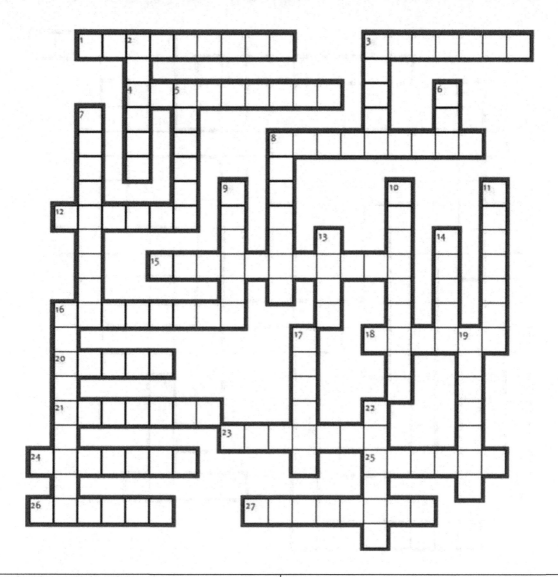

Across	Genesis 45-47
1.	Jacob and all his ___ went to Egypt. 46:6
3.	Who did Jacob want to be buried with? 47:30
4.	Why Joseph's brothers could not answer him? 45:3
8.	Who were detestable to Egyptians. 46:34
12.	How did God speak to Israel? 46:2
15.	God saved the brother's lives by a great ___. 45:7
16.	Who was given 3-hundred shekels of silver? 45:22
18.	Whose hands would close Jacob's eyes? 46:4
20.	God made Joseph lord of all ___. 45:9
21.	Number of children born to Jacob and Zilpah? 46:18
23.	Only these people could retain their land. 47:22
24.	How many in Jacob's family went to Egypt? 46:27
25.	Who gave birth to Joseph and Benjamin? 46:19
26.	Egypt and Canaan experienced severe ___ 47:13
27.	Rachel and Jacob had how many sons? 46:22

Down	Genesis 45-47
2.	Joseph asked about his ___ 45:3
3.	How much of Egypt's produce was Pharaohs? 47:26
5.	Who was the firstborn of Jacob? 46:8
6.	Who sent Joseph ahead to Pharaoh? 45:5
7.	Joseph reduced the people of Egypt to ___. 47:21
8.	Jacob's reaction to hearing Joseph was alive. 45:26
9.	God said He would make Israel into a ___. 46:3
10.	What did Egyptians exchange for food? 47:16
11.	Who received a blessing from Jacob? 47:7
13.	What did Joseph buy for Pharaoh? 47:20
14.	Joseph asked attendants and everyone to ___. 45:1
16.	Where did Israel offer sacrifices to God? 46:1
17.	Where were the brothers to live? 45:10
19.	Pharaoh was ___ to welcome Joseph's family. 45:16
22.	Who did Joseph go to meet in Goshen? 46:29

Bible Study CrossWords

Genesis 45-47

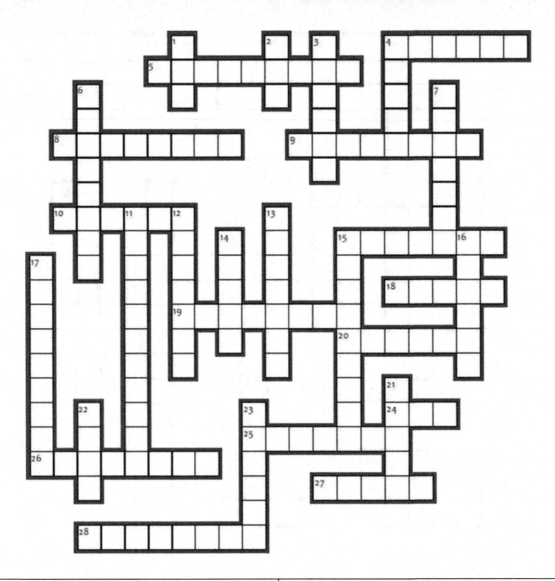

Across Genesis 48-50

4. Who Jacob called a fruitful vine. 49:22
5. In what field was Jacob buried? 50:13
8. Who did Jacob buy his burial place from? 49:32
9. Where would Zebulun live? 49:13
10. Joseph's brothers worried he held a ___. 50:15
15. Jacob wanted to be buried with his ___. 49:29
18. Who did Israel ask to bless Joseph's sons? 48:16
19. Israel gave Joseph land he took from the ___. 48:22 12.
20. Israel had how many tribes? 49:28
24. Who did Israel say was his shepherd? 48:15
25. How many days did Egyptian mourning last. 50:3
26. One of Joseph's sons. 48:1
27. How many days did it take to embalm? 50:3 17.
28. God told Jacob he would make him ___. 48:4 21.

Down Genesis 48-50

1. Who would provide justice for his people? 49:16
2. Joseph lived one-hundred and ___ years 50:26
3. Who died on the road to Ephrath? 48:7
4. Jacob said his brothers would praise ___. 49:8
6. God allowed Israel to see Joseph's ___. 48:11
7. The brothers asked Joseph to do this for them. 50:17
11. Who of Egypt went with Joseph to bury Jacob. 50:7
12. Israel put his right hand on the head of ___. 48:14
13. Joseph promised to ___ for his brothers. 50:21
14. To who did God appear at Luz? 48:3
15. Manasseh was Joseph's ___. 48:18
16. Who was the first sign of Jacob's strength? 49:3
17. Another name for Ephrath. 48:7
21. Where was Joseph's body and coffin placed? 50:26
22. Joseph called his brothers the ___ of Israel. 50:25
23. Who did Joseph and his sons visited when ill? 48:2

Bible Study CrossWords

Genesis 48-50

PROMOTIONAL PUZZLES

Because of a unique format individual BibleStudy CrossWords puzzles stand on the their own. Not requiring an answer grid means the puzzles can be promotional handouts and advertisements with a message, logo and contact information as shown in this sample.

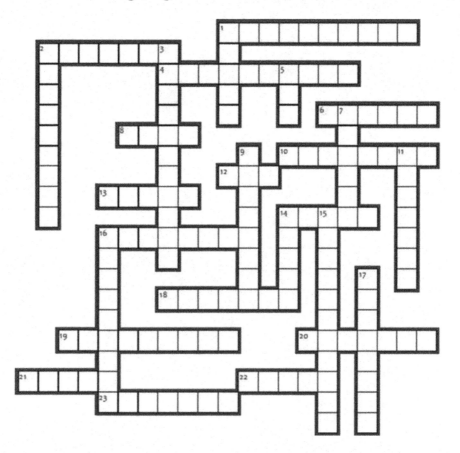

Across	Genesis 6-9
1.	The of heaven opened to create rain. 7:11
2.	Type of wood used to build the ark. 6:14
4.	What did God give Noah as food? 9:3
6.	Who Noah said to be Shem's slave. 9:26
8.	What did God use to recede the waters? 8:1
10.	God wiped every from the earth. 7:4
12.	How many hundred years was Noah? 7:6
13.	Kind of bird sent to check the water. 8:7
14.	The ark was 4-hundred and _ feet long. 6:15
16.	What the animals did after the flood? 8:17
18.	How did the waters react to the wind? 8:1
19.	How were daughters of men viewed? 6:2
20.	Noah prayed for this son's territory. 9:27
21.	Number of each clean animal. 7:2
22.	The leaf the dove brought to the ark. 8:11
23.	What month did the ark come to rest? 8:4

Down	Genesis 6-9
1.	How many days did it rain? 7:4
2.	God saw that people were ____. 6:12
3.	Day the ark came to rest. 8:4
5.	Who was the father of Canaan. 9:18
7.	Where the ark came to rest. 8:4
9.	What did Noah plant? 9:20
11.	What was the sign of God's covenant? 9:13
14.	Never again will God use this to destroy the earth. 9:11
15.	What God used to destroy life on earth. 6:17
16.	What were covered with over 20-feet of water? 7:20
17.	Who were the heroes of old, men of renown? 6:4

(MESSAGE)

YOUR LOGO & CONTACT
INFORMATION

BibleStudy CrossWords 2020

Contact Bob Meister for more information and to request personalized sample:
479-644-4518 / church7@cox.net

Printed in the United States
By Bookmasters